Contents

LIVING THINGS

MATERIALS

PHYSICAL PROCESSES

WORKING SCIENTIFICALLY

Skeletons & muscles

THE HUMAN SKELETON

Your skeleton has three jobs.

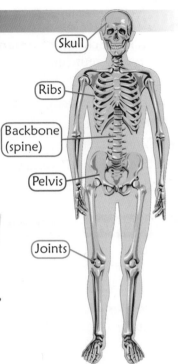

Skull

Ribs

Backbone (spine)

Pelvis

Joints

1 It supports you.
Without your skeleton you'd be very floppy.

2 It protects your important organs.
For example, your skull protects your brain and your ribs protect your heart and lungs.

3 It helps you move.
Although bones are rigid, the joints and muscles allow your skeleton to bend.

Did you know?

Many other animals have skeletons, including rabbits, dogs and whales. But some animals, such as worms, don't have any bones at all.

MUSCLES

Muscles are attached to your bones to help you move your arms and legs.

Muscles can pull bones, but they can't push them. This means muscles have to work in pairs – when one muscle contracts (gets shorter) the other relaxes.

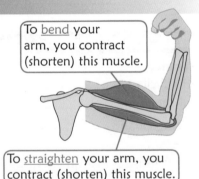

To bend your arm, you contract (shorten) this muscle.

To straighten your arm, you contract (shorten) this muscle.

QUICK QUIZ

1 For which one of these life processes are bones important?

Reproduction   Nutrition   Movement

2 Birds have hollow bones.
Why do you think this is a good thing for birds?

Your heart

WHAT YOUR HEART DOES

Your heart is a muscle. It sits in the middle of your chest, protected by your ribs. The job of your heart is to <u>pump blood</u> around your body.

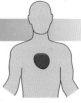

The diagram below shows that your heart first pumps blood to your <u>lungs</u> to pick up <u>oxygen</u>. Then your heart pumps the blood, along with the oxygen, to the <u>rest of your body</u>.

1. The heart pumps blood to the lungs. (The tubes that your blood travels through are called blood vessels.)

2. The blood picks up oxygen in the lungs.

3. The heart pumps blood carrying oxygen to the rest of the body. (In this diagram, blood that's carrying oxygen is coloured red.)

5. The blood returns to the heart.

4. The oxygen in the blood is used by the body.

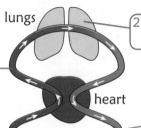

lungs

heart

body

YOUR PULSE

Your heart beats roughly 80 times per minute. Each beat pushes blood through your blood vessels, creating a <u>pulse</u>. You can feel the pulse in your <u>wrist</u> by placing two fingers alongside the base of the thumb and pressing slightly.

Exercising makes your heart beat faster
When you <u>exercise</u>, your heart <u>beats faster</u>. This is because your muscles need more oxygen, so your heart needs to <u>pump blood</u> around your body <u>more quickly</u>. After you stop exercising, your pulse rate takes a little while to get back to its resting level.

QUICK QUIZ

Helen measures her pulse rate during various activities. Match the activities to the pulse rates.

| Sitting | Walking | Running |

| 95 beats per minute | 77 beats per minute | 127 beats per minute |

The digestive system

HOW FOOD IS DIGESTED

The <u>digestive system</u> breaks down the food you eat so that your body can use it for <u>energy</u>, <u>growth</u> and <u>repair</u>.

1. Mouth
<u>Teeth</u> break food into smaller pieces.

<u>Saliva</u> helps you swallow your food and contains chemicals that start to break it down.

Your <u>tongue</u> pushes the food down your throat into your oesophagus.

2. Oesophagus
Chewed-up food travels down your oesophagus (a <u>long tube</u>) into your stomach. This part of the journey takes 5 or 6 seconds.

3. Stomach
Stomach <u>acid</u> turns the chewed-up food into a thick liquid. This travels into your small intestine after 2 to 4 hours.

4. Small intestine
<u>Digested food</u> is absorbed into your bloodstream. This takes up to 6 hours.

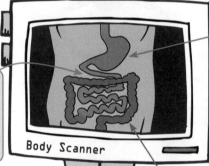

Body Scanner

Did you know? In an adult, the small intestine is around 7 metres long.

5. Large intestine
<u>Excess water</u> is absorbed back into your body. This can take 16 hours or more.

<u>Solid waste</u> passes out of your body when you go to the toilet.

QUICK QUIZ

Kris has written the stages of digestion in the wrong order. What is the correct order?

Mouth ▸ Stomach ▸ Oesophagus ▸ Large intestine ▸ Small intestine ✗

Teeth

TYPES OF TEETH

Humans have three main types of teeth: <u>incisors</u>, <u>canines</u> and <u>molars</u>. Each type does a different job.

Incisors (front teeth)
Used for cutting and snipping food.

This is the part of the tooth you can see.

This is the root.

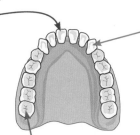

Canines (fangs)
Used for gripping and tearing food.

Molars (back teeth)
Used for crushing and chewing food.

ANIMAL TEETH

Animals that <u>only eat meat</u> are called <u>carnivores</u>. Carnivores have long, pointed <u>canine</u> teeth (fangs) that they use for gripping and tearing flesh.

Tigers have long, pointed canines.

Animals that <u>only eat plants</u> are called <u>herbivores</u>. Most herbivores don't have canine teeth, as they don't need to tear flesh. Instead, they have <u>sharp incisors</u> for <u>cutting</u> leaves or grass, and <u>large, flat molars</u> for <u>grinding and chewing</u>.

Sheep don't have any canine teeth.

Some animals don't have any teeth at all.

Worms don't have teeth (or any other hard parts in their mouths).

Birds don't have teeth – they have beaks instead.

QUICK QUIZ

1 Which of these animals does *not* have canine teeth?

Dog   Cow   Lion

2 True or false? Birds have a set of teeth inside their beaks.

Keeping healthy

LOOKING AFTER YOUR TEETH

Tooth decay is caused by bacteria. The bacteria feed on bits of food left in your mouth after you have eaten. To avoid tooth decay:

✔ Brush your teeth twice a day – first thing in the morning and last thing at night.

✔ Visit your dentist regularly. The dentist will look for any problems and stop them getting worse.

✘ Try to drink water or milk, rather than fizzy drinks.

✘ Don't eat too many sweets or sugary foods.

AVOIDING DISEASE

Diseases caused by viruses can quickly spread from person to person. To avoid spreading disease:

Someone sneezed on me.

✔ Always sneeze into a tissue.
✔ Cover your mouth with your hands when you cough.
✔ Wash your hands frequently.

FOOD HYGIENE

Eating mouldy food can make you ill. But even food that looks, tastes and smells okay may contain harmful bacteria. Make sure you:

✔ Wash your hands before touching food.
✔ Keep cold foods in a fridge (to slow down the growth of bacteria).
✔ Heat food properly (to kill any bacteria).

✘ Do not let cooked foods come into contact with raw meat.

QUICK QUIZ

1 Why do you think it is a bad idea to eat anything after you have cleaned your teeth at night?

2 Why do surgeons wear face masks when operating?

Keeping healthy

EAT A HEALTHY DIET

Your diet is what you eat. To stay healthy you should eat a <u>balanced diet</u> which includes a <u>mixture of foods</u> from these three groups:

FOOD FOR GROWTH
These foods help your body <u>grow and repair</u> itself:

Nuts

Seeds

 Fish

 Meat

 Eggs

Lentils

 Beans

Cheese

Milk

FOOD FOR ENERGY
Foods containing <u>starch</u> or <u>sugar</u> give you <u>fuel for activity</u>.

 Cereals

Rice

Bread

 COLA

Cakes & biscuits

Potatoes

Pasta

Fizzy drinks

 Sweets

<u>Fats and oils</u> provide energy which your body can <u>store</u> and use later.

⚠ Don't eat too many sugary or fatty foods.

 Milk

 Meat

Cheese

Butter

Cooking oil

FOOD FOR HEALTH
<u>Vegetables</u>, <u>fruit</u> and <u>cereals</u> contain <u>fibre</u>, which keeps your digestive system healthy.

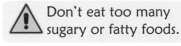

You need <u>vitamins and minerals</u> from foods such as <u>fruit</u>, <u>vegetables</u>, <u>milk</u> and <u>fish</u>. Vitamins and minerals keep you healthy. For example, milk contains calcium which helps keep your bones strong.

EXERCISE REGULARLY

As well as eating a balanced diet, you should exercise every day to stay healthy. Exercise <u>strengthens</u> your <u>muscles</u> (including your <u>heart</u>) and your <u>bones</u>.

Keeping healthy

MEDICINES ARE DRUGS

A drug is a substance that changes your physical or mental state. <u>Medicines are drugs</u> that are used to <u>treat or prevent diseases</u>.

Some medicines can have unwanted <u>side effects</u>. For example, some medicines for hayfever can make you sleepy. However, people who suffer from hayfever may prefer to be sleepy than sneezy!

 Medicine always comes with instructions, telling you how much to take and when to take it. Always <u>follow the instructions</u>, otherwise the treatment may not work or could cause you harm.

TOBACCO, ALCOHOL & OTHER DRUGS

Some people <u>smoke</u>, <u>drink alcohol</u> or <u>take other drugs</u> for pleasure. However, smoking, drinking and taking drugs have serious <u>health risks</u>.

TOBACCO contains a drug called nicotine which makes smoking addictive (hard to give up). <u>Smoking is very bad for you.</u> It can cause lung cancer, heart disease and other nasty illnesses.

 Breathing other people's smoke is called <u>passive smoking</u>. Passive smoking can also damage your heart and lungs.

ALCOHOL is a drug found in drinks like beer and wine. Alcohol slows down your reactions and can make you do silly things. Drinking too much alcohol in one go can make you feel ill.

 <u>Regularly drinking a lot is bad for you.</u> It can damage your liver, heart, brain and stomach.

QUICK QUIZ

1 You can improve your diet by varying the colours of fruit and vegetables you eat. Think of one fruit and one vegetable that is each of these colours:
   a Orange   **b** Green   **c** Yellow   **d** Red
2 Kirsty has a ham and cheese sandwich for lunch. She has fish and chips for tea. How could Kirsty improve her diet?
3 True or false? All drugs are bad for you.

Life cycles

THE HUMAN LIFE CYCLE

Adults have babies. These babies grow into adults which in turn have babies of their own. This process is called the human life cycle.

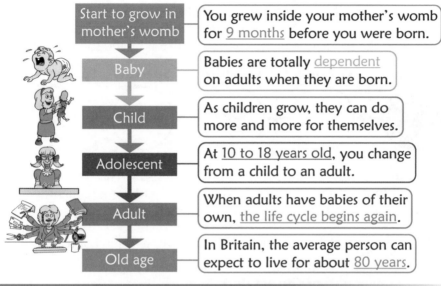

Start to grow in mother's womb	You grew inside your mother's womb for 9 months before you were born.
Baby	Babies are totally dependent on adults when they are born.
Child	As children grow, they can do more and more for themselves.
Adolescent	At 10 to 18 years old, you change from a child to an adult.
Adult	When adults have babies of their own, the life cycle begins again.
Old age	In Britain, the average person can expect to live for about 80 years.

LIFE CYCLES OF OTHER ANIMALS

Most mammals (including humans) give birth to live young. Some other animals lay eggs, for example birds, amphibians (frogs and toads) and insects.

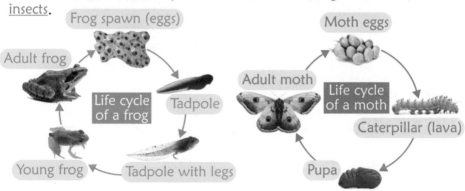

Frog spawn (eggs)

Adult frog

Life cycle of a frog

Tadpole

Young frog

Tadpole with legs

Moth eggs

Adult moth

Life cycle of a moth

Caterpillar (lava)

Pupa

See page 15 for the life cycle of a flowering plant.

QUICK QUIZ

Put these phases for an animal life cycle in the correct order.

Growth   Death   Reproduction   Birth

Food chains

A food chain can be used to show the feeding relationships between plants and animals. It basically shows what eats what.

In the food chain below, each arrow means 'is eaten by'. So the rosebush is eaten by the greenfly, the greenfly is eaten by the ladybird, the ladybird is eaten by the sparrow and the sparrow is eaten by the sparrowhawk.

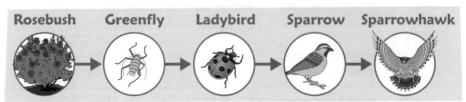

Rosebush → Greenfly → Ladybird → Sparrow → Sparrowhawk

Notice that the food chain starts with a green plant. This is the case for nearly all food chains. Plants make their own food using sunlight, water and air – they don't eat other plants or animals.

Note If one part of a food chain alters, the whole chain is affected.

What would happen if a disease suddenly killed half of the ladybirds?

- There would be fewer sparrows because they would have less to eat, so some would starve.
- There would be fewer sparrowhawks because there would be fewer sparrows to eat.
- There would be more greenfly because there would be fewer ladybirds eating them.
- There would be fewer rosebushes because more greenfly would be eating them.

QUICK QUIZ

1 What is wrong with this food chain?

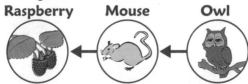

Raspberry ← Mouse ← Owl

2 Put **snail**, **thrush** and **cabbage** in the right order on this food chain.

.... → .... → ....

Food chains

PRODUCERS & CONSUMERS

Plants are called producers because they produce (make) their own food. Animals are called consumers because they consume (eat) other plants and animals.

| Grass | Rabbit | Fox |
| Producer | Consumer | Consumer |

In the food chain above, the grass is a producer because it makes its own food using sunlight, air and water. The rabbit is a consumer because it eats grass. The fox is also a consumer as it eats rabbits.

PREDATORS & PREY

A predator is an animal that eats other animals. The animals the predator eats are called its prey.

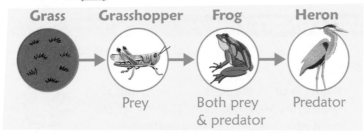

| Grass | Grasshopper | Frog | Heron |
| | Prey | Both prey & predator | Predator |

Here, the frog is both prey and predator. It's prey because frogs are eaten by herons. It's a predator because frogs eat grasshoppers.

QUICK QUIZ

Look at this food chain.

Rosebush   Greenfly   Ladybird   Sparrow   Sparrowhawk

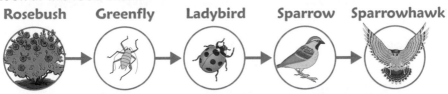

1 Are these producers or consumers? **a** Sparrow **b** Rosebush
2 True or false? The ladybird is a predator of the sparrow.
3 True or false? The rosebush is the prey of the greenfly.

Plants & growing conditions

PARTS OF A PLANT

Flowering plants have four main parts:

Flowers
Flowers are used for reproduction (see pages 13 and 14).

Leaves
Leaves make food for growth. Leaves need sunlight, air, water and warmth to make food.

Stem
The stem supports the plant. Water travels up the stem, from the roots to the leaves.

Roots
Roots anchor the plant to the ground. The roots take in water and nutrients from the soil.

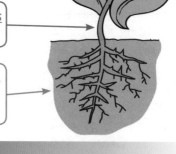

GROWING CONDITIONS

Plants need sunlight, air, water, warmth, nutrients from soil and room to grow.

Sunlight Plants kept in the dark will grow tall and spindly in search of light. Plants that get no sunlight at all will eventually die.

Air Plants need carbon dioxide gas from the air to grow well. Without it they will die.

Water A plant's leaves will dry up if it doesn't get enough water. Plants that get too much or too little water will eventually die.

Warmth Plants grow more slowly when it's cold. If it's too cold (or hot) plants won't grow at all – they'll die.

QUICK QUIZ

1 True or false? A plant takes in food through its roots.
2 Why is the South Pole <u>not</u> a good place to grow plants?

How plants reproduce

PARTS OF A FLOWER

Stigma
The stigma is the top of the female part of the flower. It's sticky to catch grains of pollen.

Stamens
Stamens are the male parts of the flower. They make pollen (fine yellow powder).

Style
The style supports the stigma.

Petals
Petals are often brightly coloured to attract insects.

Sepals
Sepals are leaves that protect the flower while it is still in bud.

Ovary
The ovary contains the ovules (eggs).

POLLINATION

Pollination is when pollen is transferred from the stamen of one flower to the stigma of another. The pollen can be carried by insects or blown by the wind. Pollination is the start of the reproduction process.

Pollination by insects
Brightly coloured flowers make a sweet liquid called nectar for insects to feed on. When insects crawl inside the flower to get the nectar, they get covered in pollen from the stamens. At the next flower they visit, the pollen gets stuck to the sticky stigma.

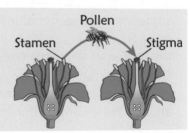

Pollen

Stamen   Stigma

Pollination by the wind
Flowers that are pollinated by the wind do *not* need to be attractive to insects. Instead, the pollen grains need to be very small and light so they can be blown from the stamen of one flower to the stigma of another.

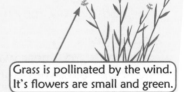

Grass is pollinated by the wind. It's flowers are small and green.

QUICK QUIZ

Do you think this flower is pollinated by insects or by the wind? How do you know?

How plants reproduce

SEED FORMATION

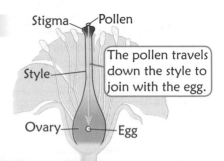

Fertilisation comes after pollination

The pollen travels down the style to the ovary. In the ovary, the pollen and the egg join. This is called fertilisation. After fertilisation, the egg becomes a seed and the ovary turns into the fruit.

Stigma   Pollen

The pollen travels down the style to join with the egg.

Style

Ovary   Egg

SEED DISPERSAL

If all new plants started growing next to their parent plant, they wouldn't have enough space, light, air, water or nutrients to survive. To avoid this overcrowding, plants disperse (scatter) their seeds over a large area. Seeds can be dispersed by wind, animals, water and even explosion!

Seed dispersal by wind

Some seeds are light and feathery so they are easily blown away by the wind. For example, dandelion seeds.

Other seeds have 'wings' to help them fly a long way from the parent plant. For example, sycamore seeds.

Seed dispersal by animals

Sometimes the seeds are inside a tasty fruit. For example, pips in apples and berries. Animals eat the fruit, and the seeds end up in their droppings.

Some seeds have tiny hooks that can catch on fur or feathers. The seeds are then carried away by the animal. For example, burdock seeds.

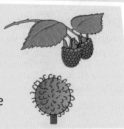

Seed dispersal by explosion

Some seeds, for example peas, grow in pods. When the pods dry up, they twist and fire out the seeds.

Seed dispersal by water

Some plants grow near water. Seeds can be carried a long way from the parent plant in streams, rivers or even the sea.

QUICK QUIZ

1 Pollen joins with an egg. Is this pollination or fertilisation?
2 Why do seeds need to be dispersed?

How seeds grow into plants

GERMINATION

Germination is when a seed starts to grow into a new plant. Seeds need water, warmth and air for germination, but they do not need light.

 Don't forget | Plants need light to make food. However, seeds contain enough food to start growing (germinate), so they do not need light to begin with.

Stage 1 The seed opens and a root grows downwards.	**Stage 2** A tiny shoot grows upwards.	**Stage 3** The plant grows leaves so it can start making its own food.

LIFE CYCLE OF FLOWERING PLANTS

The diagram below is a summary of the life cycle of flowering plants:

 Seed

Seed dispersal
The seeds are spread away from the plant.

Germination
The seed starts to grow into a plant.

Seed formation
Pollen joins with the egg. The fertilised eggs then become seeds.

 **Young plant**

Plant grows
Plants need sunlight, air, water, warmth, nutrients and room to grow.

Pollination
Pollen is transferred from one flower to another.

 Plant with flowers

QUICK QUIZ

What does a seed need to start growing? What is this process called?

Habitats

WHAT IS A HABITAT?

A habitat is the place where a plant or animal lives.
Examples of habitats are seashores, meadows, deserts, jungles and lakes.

The picture shows a woodland habitat.
The plants and animals living in this
habitat include grass, trees, rabbits, foxes,
deer, birds, worms and woodlice.

A micro-habitat is a very small habitat,
such as the space under a stone or log
where the woodlice live.

PLANTS & ANIMALS ARE ADAPTED TO THEIR HABITATS

Plants and animals have special features
that help them survive in their habitats.

**A cactus is adapted to
a hot, dry habitat**

**Giraffes are adapted to open
grassland with scattered trees**

Tough lips protect it when
eating leaves from prickly trees.

Giraffes are very tall, so they
can reach leaves in tall trees.

Strong back legs give a
powerful kick that protects
the giraffe from lions.

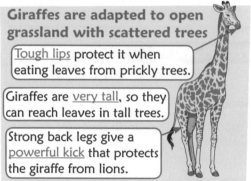

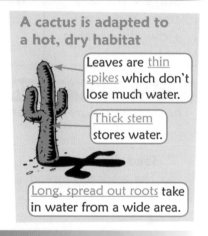

Leaves are thin
spikes which don't
lose much water.

Thick stem
stores water.

Long, spread out roots take
in water from a wide area.

HABITATS CAN CHANGE

Habitats can change and this can pose dangers to
plants and animals that live there. For example,
new reservoirs and dams may change river habitats.
Changes to flow rates or oxygen levels in a river can
make it difficult for certain types of fish to survive.

QUICK QUIZ

Match these animals with their habitats and special features.

Camel Pond Long, thick eyelashes to keep out sand

Frog Arctic Thick fur to keep warm

Polar bear Desert Webbed feet for swimming

Evolution & inheritance

Evolution explains how plants and animals have changed over time. All plants and animals have evolved from simple life forms.

Evidence for evolution comes from fossils (see page 20). Fossils of the simplest life forms are found in the oldest rocks, and fossils of more advanced life forms are found in newer rocks.

FOSSILS SHOW THAT HORSES HAVE EVOLVED

Modern horses have evolved from small, dog-sized creatures. We know this because we have found fossils from the main stages of horse evolution. The age of the fossils tells us that this evolution took many millions of years.

DEER MICE HAVE EVOLVED TO BLEND IN

Deer mice usually live in woods. The mice are normally dark brown, so they can blend into their dark surroundings and hide from predators.

Some deer mice, however, have ended up living in sand-dunes. Most baby mice are the same colour as their parents, but some will be slightly lighter or darker. As the paler mice were better camouflaged in the sandy habitat, more of them survived and had babies of their own. (The darker mice were easier for predators to spot.)

Eventually the deer mice that live in the sand-dunes evolved to be sandy coloured.

ARCTIC FOXES HAVE EVOLVED TO KEEP WARM

Arctic foxes live in the very cold climate of the Arctic. To help them survive the cold, they have evolved to have thick coats of insulating fur.

This evolution happened over many, many years. Cubs who grew thicker coats were more likely to survive and have cubs of their own. As cubs inherit characteristics from their parents, more and more cubs had thicker and thicker coats.

QUICK QUIZ

What is likely to happen to an animal that is poorly suited to its habitat?

Classification keys

HOW TO USE A KEY

A key is a <u>series of questions</u> that helps you identify living things.

The key below can be used to decide whether a <u>squirrel</u> is a fish, reptile, bird, mammal or amphibian.

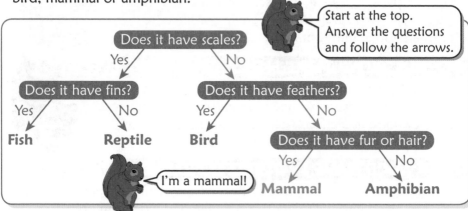

Start at the top. Answer the questions and follow the arrows.

Does it have scales?
Yes / No

Does it have fins?
Yes / No

Does it have feathers?
Yes / No

Fish   **Reptile**   **Bird**

Does it have fur or hair?
Yes / No

I'm a mammal!   **Mammal**   **Amphibian**

Here is a key that helps you identify <u>snakes</u>:

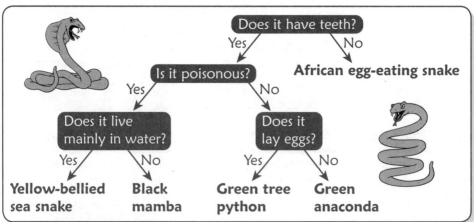

Does it have teeth?
Yes / No

African egg-eating snake

Is it poisonous?
Yes / No

Does it live mainly in water?
Yes / No

Does it lay eggs?
Yes / No

Yellow-bellied sea snake   **Black mamba**   **Green tree python**   **Green anaconda**

From the key above, you can see that a <u>green tree python</u> has <u>teeth</u>, is <u>not poisonous</u> and <u>lays eggs</u>.

QUICK QUIZ

1 Use the key at the top of the page.
   What group does this animal belong to?
2 Look at the second key.
   Write down three facts about a black mamba.

Rocks & soil

ROCKS

Rocks are everywhere under the ground. Some rocks are harder than others, which makes them useful for different jobs. For example:

Granite is a hard rock. Steps are often made from granite as it doesn't wear away easily.

Marble is a hard rock. Marble is often used to make statues as it looks nice and lasts a long time.

Slate is a hard rock. Slate is often used for roof tiles as it can be split into thin sheets and doesn't let water through.

Chalk is a soft rock. It's good for drawing because it wears away easily, leaving a mark.

Some rocks let water through and some don't. Rocks that let water through are called permeable rocks. For example, chalk is a permeable rock. Granite, marble and slate are not permeable rocks.

SOIL

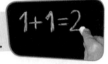

Soil is made from tiny particles of rock mixed with decayed plants and animals. It also contains air and water.

Different types of rock make different types of soil. For example:

Sandy soil is pale and feels gritty. Water drains through sandy soil easily, as there are lots of small air gaps.

Clay soil feels lumpy and sticky when it's very wet. Water does not drain through clay soil very quickly. When it dries out it goes very hard and cracks.

Chalky soil is usually stony. Water drains through chalky soil quickly.

QUICK QUIZ

1 Why is chalk not a suitable material for roof tiles? Give two reasons.
2 Rock A is rubbed against Rock B. Pieces of Rock A are worn away. One of the rocks is chalk and one is marble. Which is which?

Rocks & fossils

SEDIMENTARY ROCK

Sediment is a naturally occurring material that is broken down by weather and erosion, and is carried by the wind, water or glaciers. Sand and gravel are types of sediment.

As more and more sediment settles, it gets pressed together and eventually becomes rock. This can take many millions of years.

Limestone, chalk and shale are examples of sedimentary rocks.

 Over 2 million blocks of limestone were used to make The Great Pyramid of Giza in Egypt.

FOSSILS

A fossil is the preserved remains or impression of a dead plant or animal. Fossils are often found in sedimentary rocks.

Bones, shells and leaves can be covered by sediment. Eventually the bones, shells and leaves are replaced by minerals and become rock.

Fossils are often so small that they need to be viewed under a microscope. Large, well-preserved fossils are relatively rare.

Dead plants and animals can also be preserved in amber (fossilised tree resin).

Footprints of animals can also be covered by sediment. When the sediment becomes rock, the footprint is preserved as a fossil.

QUICK QUIZ

Sedimentary rock is formed in layers. In a cliff made from sedimentary rock, where do you think the oldest layer is usually found?

At the bottom   In the middle   At the top

Conducting heat & electricity

CONDUCTING HEAT

Thermal conductors

Heat travels through some materials easily. These materials are called thermal conductors. Metals are good thermal conductors.

Saucepans need to conduct heat well, so they are usually made from metal.

Thermal insulators

Heat *does not* travel through some materials easily. These materials are called thermal insulators. Good thermal insulators include polystyrene, cork, plastic and wood.

An insulated flask keeps hot drinks hot. The same flask can be used to keep cold drinks cold by keeping heat out.

Woolly clothes are good thermal insulators. They stop the heat escaping from your body.

Wooden spoons don't get hot because wood is a poor conductor.

CONDUCTING ELECTRICITY

Electrical conductors

Electricity travels through some materials easily. These materials are called electrical conductors. Metals are good electrical conductors.

Electrical insulators

Materials that do not let electricity flow through them are called electrical insulators. Plastic is a good electrical insulator.

Electricity passes through the metal key and lights up the bulb.

Electricity cannot pass through the plastic toothbrush, so the bulb doesn't light up.

QUICK QUIZ

1 Aluminium is a good conductor of heat.
  Is aluminium a good thermal insulator or a poor thermal insulator?
2 Why are the wires in a circuit coated with plastic?
3 What would happen if you replaced the key in the circuit above with a wooden ruler?

Solids, liquids & gases

SOLIDS

Wood, plastic and ice are examples of solids. You can tell they are solids because you can grab hold of them. Solids can also be cut or shaped.

When you put a solid in a container, it does not spread out. It stays the same shape.

Even though sugar, salt and rice can be poured, they are still solids. Each individual grain stays the same shape.

LIQUIDS

Examples of liquids include water, milk and shampoo. Liquids are runny and can be poured easily.

A liquid takes the shape of the bottom of its container.

When you tilt the bottle, the surface of the liquid stays level. Although the shape of the liquid changes, it still takes up the same amount of space (volume).

GASES

Gases are often invisible. For example, air is a mixture of different gases. You cannot see air, but you can feel it when it's windy.

A gas spreads out to fill its container. The gas takes the same shape and volume as the container.

When you take the cork out of the bottle, the gas escapes and spreads out.

QUICK QUIZ

1 Decide whether these are solids, liquids or gases.

Vinegar   Chalk   Flour   Helium inside a balloon

2 True or false? Only liquids can be poured.

Hot & cold

Temperature tells you how hot or cold something is.
You can use a thermometer like this to measure temperature:

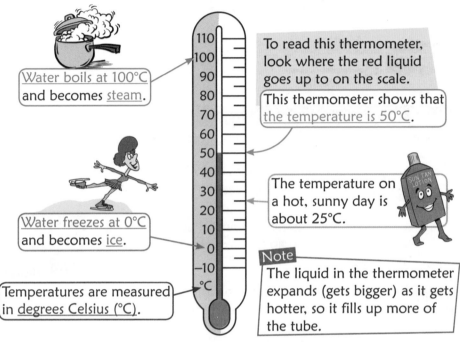

Water boils at 100°C and becomes steam.

To read this thermometer, look where the red liquid goes up to on the scale.

This thermometer shows that the temperature is 50°C.

The temperature on a hot, sunny day is about 25°C.

Water freezes at 0°C and becomes ice.

Temperatures are measured in degrees Celsius (°C).

Note
The liquid in the thermometer expands (gets bigger) as it gets hotter, so it fills up more of the tube.

HOT THINGS COOL DOWN ...

Hot things cool down until they are the same temperature as their surroundings.

For example, if you don't drink a hot drink straight away, it cools down. It keeps cooling down until it's the same temperature as the air in the room.

Similarly, cold things warm up until they are the same temperature as their surroundings.

QUICK QUIZ

1 Match these items with their temperatures:

    Bath water   Ice lolly   Glass of cold milk   −2°C   38°C   5°C

2 How could you keep a hot drink warm for longer?

Changing state

Materials can change between being a solid, a liquid or a gas.
For example, water (a liquid) can freeze to become a solid (ice).
Water can also evaporate to become a gas (water vapour).

SOLID — Melting → LIQUID — Evaporation → GAS
Freezing ← Condensation ←

MELTING

Melting is what happens when a solid turns into a liquid.

For example, a solid ice cube melts to become water.

In a warmer room, the ice cube will melt faster.

Even metals will melt if you heat them up enough. Gold turns into a liquid at a temperature of 1064°C. That's really hot!

Did you know? Not all metals are solid at room temperature. The metal mercury is a liquid!

FREEZING (SOLIDIFYING)

Freezing is what happens when a liquid turns into a solid.
Freezing is the opposite of melting.

For example, on a very cold day, water will freeze to become ice.

Freezing is sometimes called solidifying.

Did you know? Many chocolate shapes are made by pouring melted chocolate into a mould. The liquid chocolate takes the shape of the mould. As the chocolate cools down it solidifies (turns back into a solid) and keeps its new shape.

Note Freezing and melting are called reversible changes because they can be reversed or undone (see page 27).

Changing state

EVAPORATION

Evaporation is what happens when a liquid turns into a gas.

Wet clothes become dry when you hang them on a washing line. The water in the clothes evaporates into a gas (water vapour) and is then carried away by the air.

(In warmer weather, evaporation is faster, so clothes dry quicker.)

 When you open a bottle of perfume the liquid evaporates into a gas. You can smell the perfume when the gas reaches your nose.

When you heat water to 100°C, the water evaporates so fast that bubbles of water vapour form in the water and rise rapidly to the surface. This is called boiling.

CONDENSATION

Condensation is what happens when a gas turns into a liquid. Condensation is the opposite of evaporation.

You can see condensation in action when you have a hot bath or shower. The water vapour cools on your bathroom mirror and condenses into tiny droplets of water.

Note Evaporation and condensation are called reversible changes because they can be reversed or undone (see page 27).

QUICK QUIZ

1 Jo heats a bar of chocolate in a pan. What happens to the chocolate?
2 Match these changes of state with their names:

Water turns to water vapour   Ice turns to water   Water vapour turns to water   Water turns to ice

Melting   Freezing   Evaporation   Condensation

The water cycle

The water you drink was once in the sea. It evaporated from the sea then condensed to become a cloud. The water in the cloud fell as rain, which was collected in lakes and reservoirs. It was then cleaned before coming out of your tap. Eventually the water gets back to the sea and begins its journey again. This recycling process is called the water cycle.

You can follow the water's journey around the diagram below.

2 Water vapour condenses to form clouds. Clouds are made up of tiny water droplets.

3 Water in the clouds falls as rain. It will turn to snow if it is cold enough.

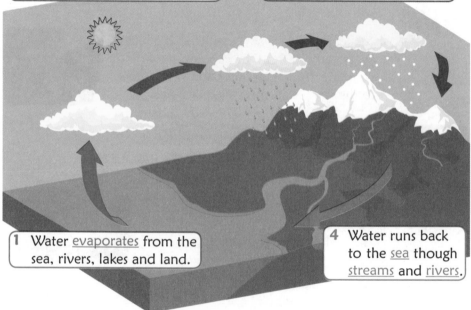

1 Water evaporates from the sea, rivers, lakes and land.

4 Water runs back to the sea though streams and rivers.

 Did you know? Water has been going round the water cycle a very long time. So you could be drinking the same water that dinosaurs drank!

Don't forget Evaporation and condensation play a big part in the water cycle. (See page 25 for more on evaporation and condensation.)

QUICK QUIZ

1 What are clouds made from: smoke, water droplets or cotton wool?

2 True or false? Water flows from the sea, up rivers to your tap.

Reversible & irreversible changes

REVERSIBLE CHANGES

Sometimes when you change a material, you can change it back again. For example, you can freeze water to turn it from a liquid to a solid (ice). You can change the ice back into a liquid by heating it. Changes that can be undone are called reversible changes.

The changes of state (melting, freezing, evaporating and condensing) are all reversible changes. (See pages 24 and 25.)

Dissolving a solid into a liquid is another example of a reversible change. You can get the solid back by evaporating. (See pages 29 and 30.)

IRREVERSIBLE CHANGES

Some changes to materials cannot be undone. Changes that cannot be reversed are called irreversible changes.

When you burn wood you get ash and smoke. Ash and smoke are new materials made by burning. You cannot change the ash and smoke back to wood, so this is an irreversible change.

When you fry an egg, the clear runny liquid changes into a white solid. The yellow yolk will also change from a liquid to a solid if you cook it long enough. You cannot change the cooked egg back into a raw egg, so this is an irreversible change.

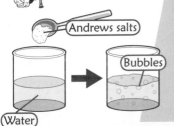

Plaster of Paris is a powder. When you mix it with water, a reaction takes place and hard plaster is produced. This change is irreversible. You cannot get the plaster of Paris powder back.

When you add Andrews salts to water, the mixture fizzes. The bubbles of gas are a new material, which is released into the air. You can't put the gas back into the mixture, so this is an irreversible change.

A similar irreversible change happens when you add vinegar to bicarbonate of soda.

QUICK QUIZ

Are these changes reversible or irreversible?

Burning paper   Melting chocolate   Dissolving sugar in water   Cooking bread

Separating mixtures of solids

USING A SIEVE

You can use a <u>sieve</u> to separate <u>mixtures of solids</u> like sand and dried peas.

Shake the sand and pea mixture in the sieve. The <u>peas</u> are <u>too big</u> to pass through the holes and remain in the sieve.

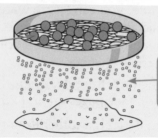

The grains of <u>sand</u> are <u>small enough</u> to pass through the holes.

Note Sieves come with <u>different sized holes</u>. You need to choose the right sieve for the solids you are separating. The holes need to be <u>small enough</u> to trap one of the solids but <u>large enough</u> to let the other solid through.

A MIXTURE OF SEVERAL SOLIDS

This is how you would separate a mixture of <u>steel paper clips</u>, <u>dried peas</u>, <u>rice</u> and <u>sand</u>:

1 Use a <u>magnet</u> to remove the <u>paper clips</u>.

2 Use a <u>sieve</u> to trap the <u>peas</u>, but let the rice and sand through.

3 Use a sieve with <u>smaller holes</u> to trap the <u>rice</u>.

Don't forget The magnet picks up the paper clips because they are made of <u>steel</u>, which is a <u>magnetic material</u>. (See page 41.)

QUICK QUIZ

1 How would you separate a mixture of steel nails, flour and marbles?

2 Why can't you use a sieve to separate sand and salt?

Separating solids & liquids

DISSOLVING SOLIDS IN LIQUIDS

Some solids dissolve when you mix them with water. For example sugar, salt and instant coffee all dissolve in water. When a solid dissolves, it makes a clear liquid called a solution.

Sugar dissolves in water to make a solution (clear liquid).

Add sugar to water and stir.

The solution is clear. You can't see any sugar, but it's still there. If you drank some, it would taste sweet. (⚠ Only taste liquids you know are safe.)

Some solids do NOT dissolve when you mix them with water. For example sand, flour and chalk do not dissolve in water. You can still see bits of the solid in the water.

Sand does NOT dissolve in water.

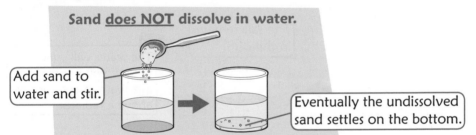

Add sand to water and stir.

Eventually the undissolved sand settles on the bottom.

FILTERING

You can use filter paper to separate solids that have NOT dissolved in water. For example, you can use filter paper to separate sand and water. Filter paper has tiny holes in it. The water can get through these holes, but the sand can't.

Filter paper

Mixture of sand and water

Funnel

The water drips through the filter paper, but the sand is left behind.

Note

You can't use a sieve to separate sand and water because the larger holes would let the sand through.

Separating solids & liquids

SEPARATING SOLUTIONS

You **cannot** separate a dissolved solid from a solution by filtering.

When a solid like salt dissolves in water, it makes a clear solution. The solid breaks down into really small pieces that you can't see. These pieces are so tiny that they would go through the holes in the filter paper.

You **can** separate a dissolved solid from a solution by evaporating.

To separate salt from a salt solution:
Step 1 Pour the solution into a wide dish.
Step 2 Wait for the water to evaporate.
The water that evaporates is pure water. None of the salt evaporates – it remains in the dish.

(The water evaporates.)

(The salt remains in the dish.)

Tip
The water will evaporate faster if you put the dish in a warm place, such as above a radiator.

(Solution of salt and water)

Did you know? Some people cook with sea salt. You get sea salt from sea water by evaporating off the water.

QUICK QUIZ

1 Which of these dissolve in water?

sand   salt   chalk   flour   sugar   instant coffee

2 Match each mixture with the quickest method of separation.

sugar and water   flour and water   paper clips and marbles   marbles and water

magnet   evaporation   sieving   filtering

3 **Challenge**
   How could you separate a mixture of salt and sand?

Electrical circuits

We get electricity from the mains or from batteries.

These use mains electricity:

These use electricity from batteries:

 Mains electricity can be very dangerous. If you are not careful, you could get an electric shock which could kill you. Always follow these rules:

- Never poke your fingers or anything else into mains sockets.
- When plugging and unplugging appliances, always hold the plastic part of the plug – never touch the metal prongs.
- Keep electrical appliances away from water.
- Don't touch switches with wet hands.

WHAT IS AN ELECTRICAL CIRCUIT?

A circuit needs a power source (such as a battery), wires and at least one other component (such as a bulb or buzzer).

Electricity can only travel around a circuit if there are no gaps.

Connect the wires to both the positive and negative ends of the battery.

 Never open a battery, as the chemicals inside are dangerous.

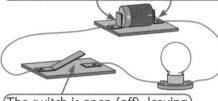

The switch is open (off), leaving a gap in the circuit. Electricity cannot travel around the circuit.

The switch is now closed (on). There is no gap in the circuit and the bulb is lit up.

QUICK QUIZ

What's wrong with these circuits?

a

b

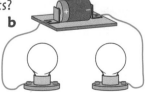

c

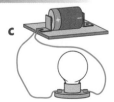

Circuit diagrams

This is a picture of a circuit. It would take ages to draw this.

It's much quicker to draw a circuit diagram using symbols.

The last column in the table below shows the symbols you should use when you draw a circuit diagram.

Draw the wires as straight lines.

Component	Picture	Symbol
Battery (cell)		⊣⊢
Two batteries		⊣⊦⊢
Wire		——
Open switch (off)		—o͜ o—
Closed switch (on)		—o—o—
Light bulb		—⊗—
Buzzer		
Motor		—(M)—

M is for Motor!

QUICK QUIZ

Use symbols to draw a circuit diagram of this circuit.

Tip Start by drawing the symbol for the battery, then work your way around the circuit in an anticlockwise direction ↺.

Changing circuits

CHANGING THE NUMBER OF BATTERIES OR BULBS

If you want to make bulbs brighter (or buzzers louder), you'll need to change the components in your circuit.

Start with a simple circuit.

Adding another battery makes the bulb brighter.
There is more electricity going round the circuit.

Adding another bulb makes the bulbs dimmer.
The bulbs have to share the electricity.

If you add too many batteries to a circuit you risk 'blowing' some of the components.

CHANGING THE WIRE

Another thing you can change in a circuit is the wire itself.

The thicker the wire, the brighter the bulb.

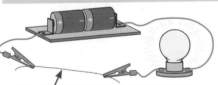

This is a very <u>thin</u> piece of wire.

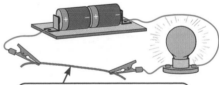

This is a <u>thicker</u> piece of wire.

The shorter the wire, the brighter the bulb.

This is a <u>long</u> piece of wire.

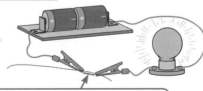

Here, the electricity only travels through this <u>short</u> bit of the wire.

Sound & musical instruments

SOUNDS ARE VIBRATIONS

Sounds are made when objects vibrate. For example, when you pluck a guitar string it vibrates and creates a sound. Any object that makes a sound is vibrating, even if you can't see the vibrations.

When something makes a sound, it makes the air around it vibrate. You hear the sound when the vibrations in the air reach your ears and make your eardrums vibrate.

SOUND NEEDS SOMETHING TO TRAVEL THROUGH

Sound can travel through

● gases such as air,

● liquids such as water, ◄——— This is why you can hear muffled sounds under the water when you are swimming.

● solids such as glass, bricks and wood. ◄——— This is why you can hear sounds through walls and windows.

Sound can't travel through a vacuum (a space with nothing in it, not even air). This is because there's nothing to pass on the vibrations.

PITCH & LOUDNESS

The pitch of a sound is how high or low it is.
The loudness of a sound is how loud or quiet (soft) it is.

Try this!

Blow across the top of a bottle with a small amount of water in it. You will hear a sound – this is the air in the bottle vibrating.

Add a bit more water and try again. You should notice that the sound is now a higher pitch. This is because there is less air in the bottle to vibrate.

Blowing harder produces stronger vibrations, which gives a louder sound.

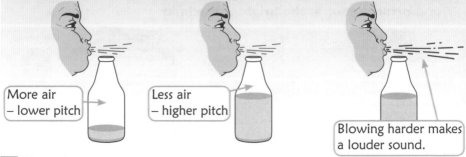

More air – lower pitch

Less air – higher pitch

Blowing harder makes a louder sound.

Sound & musical instruments

XYLOPHONES & GLOCKENSPIELS

These instruments have different length bars.
The shorter bars make higher pitched sounds.
To make a louder sound you hit the bars harder.

Note The sound is fainter if you are further away.

DRUMS

Different sized drums make different sounds.
Smaller drums make higher pitched sounds.

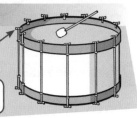

You can tighten the drum skin with these
screws. A tighter skin gives a higher pitch.

GUITARS

A guitar usually has six strings. Each
string is a different thickness. Thinner
strings give higher pitched notes.

You can tighten the strings
with these tuning keys. Tighter
strings give a higher pitch.

You can shorten the strings by
pressing your fingers on the
neck (fingerboard) of the guitar.
Shorter strings give a higher pitch.

WIND INSTRUMENTS

Wind instruments are musical instruments that you blow
into, like a recorder or penny whistle. You change the
pitch by covering some of the holes with your fingers.
This changes the amount of air that is vibrating.

QUICK QUIZ

1 Ben hits a cymbal and it makes a sound. How can he stop the sound?
2 An astronaut bangs a drum on the moon. Can she hear it?
3 Which drum will have the lower pitch?   A   B

Light & seeing

SOURCES OF LIGHT

A <u>light source</u> makes its <u>own light</u>. Here are some light sources:

The Sun	Stars	Electric lights	Candles and flames
		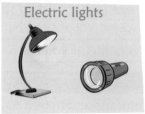	

 Looking at the Sun can damage your eyes. Don't do it!

Mirrors, metals and other shiny objects are NOT light sources. They may seem bright, but they are just <u>reflecting</u> light from another source.

These are NOT light sources:

The Moon   Mirrors

HOW YOU SEE THINGS

You see a <u>light source</u> when light from the source goes into your eyes.

Light travels in a <u>straight line</u> from the candle flame to Ben's eyes.

Ben
light source

You see an <u>object that is not a light source</u> when light bounces off the object and goes into your eyes.

Ben can see the present because it <u>reflects</u> light from the sun into his eyes.

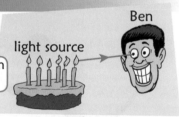
light source
Ben
object

Some objects reflect light better than others. Smooth, shiny objects reflect light better than dull, dark objects.

Mirrors are great at reflecting light.

Light & seeing

TRANSPARENT, TRANSLUCENT & OPAQUE

Some materials let light pass through them. Other materials block light.

Transparent materials
Light passes straight through transparent materials, like clear glass. You can see clearly through transparent materials.

Translucent materials
Translucent materials let some light through. You cannot see clearly through translucent materials, like some bathroom windows.

Opaque materials
Opaque materials, like metal and wood, do not let light through. You cannot see through opaque materials.

SHADOWS

When an object blocks light it creates a shadow behind it.

The shadow is formed because light can only travel in straight lines, and it can't go through the opaque object (the duck).

If you move the object further away from the light source, the shadow gets smaller.

Note Transparent objects do not make shadows because light travels straight through them.

QUICK QUIZ

Which of these statements are TRUE and which are FALSE?

1 A television screen is a source of light.
2 'Cat's eyes' on a road are a source of light.
3 A brick wall is transparent.
4 The length of your shadow is always the same as your height.

Forces

PUSHING & PULLING

A <u>force</u> is a <u>push</u> or a <u>pull</u>. You can show the <u>direction</u> of a force with an <u>arrow</u>:

Push

Pull

The man is <u>pushing</u> the car <u>forwards</u>. The harder he pushes the car, the faster it goes.

The man is <u>pulling</u> the sword <u>upwards</u>.

OPPOSITE FORCES

When you push or pull an object, you can feel the object pushing or pulling you in the opposite direction.

Push from man   Push from spring

Pull from woman   Pull from spring

The <u>man is pushing</u> the giant spring. The giant <u>spring is pushing</u> back.

The <u>woman is pulling</u> the giant spring. The <u>spring is pulling</u> back.

GRAVITY

<u>Gravity</u> is a force that <u>pulls everything down</u> towards the centre of the earth.

The force of gravity stops you falling off the Earth.

Gravity also makes rain fall towards the centre of the Earth.

Did you know?

The Moon also has gravity, but it's weaker than on the Earth because the Moon is smaller than the Earth. So you can jump higher on the Moon than on the Earth.

Forces

Levers, pulleys and gears allow a <u>smaller force</u> to have a <u>greater effect</u>.

LEVERS

This <u>lever</u> is like a <u>see-saw</u>:

> The <u>fulcrum</u> (or pivot) is a fixed support about which the bar can turn.

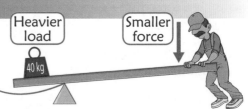

Heavier load — 40 kg — Smaller force

Because the fulcrum is <u>close to</u> the <u>heavy load</u>, it only takes a small force to lift it. An example of this type of lever is a crowbar.

A <u>wheelbarrow</u> is a type of lever where the <u>fulcrum</u> (the wheel) is at <u>the end</u>. Using a wheelbarrow, you can lift a heavier load than you would otherwise be able to.

Heavier load — Smaller force — Fulcrum

PULLEYS

This pulley system allows the man to lift a <u>heavier weight</u> using a <u>smaller force</u>. He has to pull the rope down further, but it needs less force.

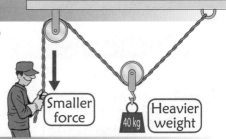

Smaller force — Heavier weight — 40 kg

GEARS

Gears are <u>wheels with teeth</u> around the edge, which mesh together.

Turning the small gear makes the large gear rotate as well, but <u>more slowly</u> and in the <u>opposite direction</u>.

Gears can help you lift heavy loads in a similar way to pulleys.

QUICK QUIZ

Which lever makes it easiest to lift the load?

A  B   C

Forces

FRICTION

Friction is a force that slows down moving objects.

For example, if you flick a coin across a desk, it is friction that slows down the coin until it stops.

Friction can also prevent objects starting to move.

For example, friction is the reason that parked cars don't slide down hills.

Smooth surfaces have less friction than rough surfaces.

For example, it is easier to slide something on a smooth wooden floor than it is on carpet.

Friction always acts in the opposite direction to the direction the object is moving in or trying to move in.

Friction

Skier moves this way

Don't forget

Friction can be very useful. Without it, cars wouldn't be able to go round bends, and you would find it impossible to walk as you wouldn't have any grip!

AIR RESISTANCE

Air resistance slows down things that are moving through the air.

Sports cars are shaped to reduce air resistance so that they can travel faster. They are said to be streamlined.

Air resistance can be a good thing. Parachutes have a large surface area which creates a lot of air resistance. This slows the parachute down.

WATER RESISTANCE

Water resistance slows down things that are moving through water. You will have felt water resistance if you have tried to walk in a swimming pool.

Fish have a streamlined shape that reduces water resistance. This helps them swim faster.

QUICK QUIZ

Why do the floor tiles around a swimming pool have a rough surface?

Magnets & magnetic materials

MAGNETIC MATERIALS

Magnets attract things made of iron.
Magnets also attract things made of steel
(steel contains iron), cobalt and nickel.

Iron and steel are
attracted to magnets.

All non-metals (e.g. plastic, wood and
rubber) are not attracted to magnets.
Metals such as aluminium and copper
are not attracted to magnets either.

Plastic and rubber are
not attracted to magnets.

 Magnets are used to sort cans for recycling.
Steel food cans are attracted to magnets,
but aluminium drinks cans are not.

MAGNETS

When you bring the ends of two magnets close together, you feel a
force pulling them together or a force pushing them apart. One end of a
magnet is called the North pole (N), the other is called the South pole (S).

Opposite poles attract
North attracts South,
and South attracts North.

Like poles repel
North repels North,
and South repels South.

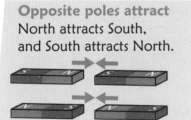

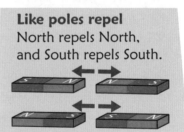

 Magnetic materials, such as iron or steel, are attracted to both
ends of a magnet. In other words, iron or steel will never be pushed
away by a magnet.

Some magnets are stronger than others. But don't be fooled –
smaller magnets can sometimes be stronger than bigger magnets.

QUICK QUIZ

Explain how you could use steel paper clips to find out which of two
magnets is the stronger.

The Earth & beyond

SUN, EARTH & MOON

The Sun, Earth and Moon are shaped roughly like giant balls (<u>spheres</u>). The diagram below shows how they travel around each other.

The Earth travels around the Sun. It takes the Earth roughly <u>365 days (1 year)</u> to orbit the Sun.

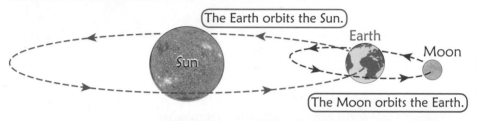

The Earth orbits the Sun.

Earth

Moon

Sun

The Moon orbits the Earth.

The Moon travels around the Earth. It takes roughly <u>28 days</u> for the Moon to orbit the Earth.

Note In real life, the Earth is roughly <u>4 times bigger</u> than the Moon. The Sun is roughly <u>100 times bigger</u> than the Earth!

DAY & NIGHT

While the Earth is travelling around the Sun, the Earth is also <u>spinning</u>. It takes <u>24 hours</u> for the Earth to spin round once. As the Earth spins:

● The half of the Earth facing the Sun is lit up by the Sun – for this half it is <u>daytime</u>.

● The other half is in darkness – for this half it is <u>night-time</u>.

As the Earth continues to spin, day turns to night.

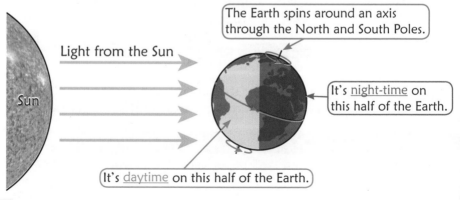

The Earth spins around an axis through the North and South Poles.

Light from the Sun

Sun

It's <u>night-time</u> on this half of the Earth.

It's <u>daytime</u> on this half of the Earth.

The Earth & beyond

THE SUN & SHADOWS

The Sun appears to move across the sky during the day. The Sun doesn't actually move – it just looks like it does because the Earth is spinning.

This is how the Sun appears to move when you're looking south:

| Morning | Midday | Evening |
| The Sun rises in the east. | The Sun is overhead. | The Sun sets in the west. |

| Shadows are long in the morning and point west. | Shadows are shortest at midday when the Sun is high in the sky. | Shadows are long in the evening and point east. |

 Never look directly at the Sun, even if you are wearing sunglasses. Look at how the shadows change instead.

THE OTHER PLANETS

The Sun is a star at the centre of our solar system.

There are 8 planets that orbit the Sun:

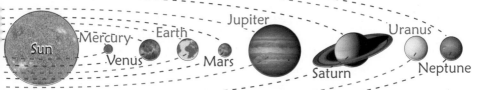

Jupiter is the biggest planet, much bigger than it looks here. Jupiter is more than 10 times bigger than the Earth.

Some of the planets have moons that orbit them. Earth has one moon, Jupiter has 4 large moons and lots of smaller moons.

QUICK QUIZ

1 True or false? It takes 24 hours for the Earth to travel round the Sun.
2 True or false? The Sun and Moon are the same size.
3 True or false? Day and night are caused by the Earth spinning.

Scientific investigations

QUESTIONS TO INVESTIGATE

At the start of a scientific investigation you need to think of a question that you would like to know the answer to.

Here are some examples of questions you could investigate:

> Does the temperature of the water make a difference to how quickly sugar dissolves?

> How does water affect plant growth?

> How does exercise affect pulse rate?

> Which surfaces give the most friction?

> On which surface does a tennis ball bounce highest?

Before you start it's a good idea to make a prediction of what you think the answer is.

CARRYING OUT A FAIR TEST

When carrying out an experiment, you should only change one factor at a time. If you change more than one factor at a time you won't know which factor affected your results.

Alesha thinks the temperature of water may affect how quickly sugar dissolves in it. She thinks these other factors may also have an effect:

- The type of sugar
- The amount of sugar
- The amount of water
- How quickly you stir it

> If you change all these factors at the same time, you won't know why the sugar dissolves quicker.

To test if sugar dissolves quicker at different water temperatures, Alesha should only change the temperature of the water. To make it a fair test, she must keep all the other factors of the experiment the same. So she must use the same type and amount of sugar each time, the same amount of water, and stir the mixture at the same speed.

EQUIPMENT & SAFETY

Before you do your experiment, think about what equipment you need to carry out your experiment safely.

Alesha decides she needs this equipment: timer, thermometer, measuring jug, teaspoon, sugar, water at different temperatures

To avoid scalding herself, she will use hot water from the tap, not boiling water from a kettle.

Scientific investigations

RECORDING YOUR RESULTS IN A TABLE

A table is a good way of recording your results. Each time you take a measurement, add it to the table.

Alesha is investigating how quickly sugar dissolves at different temperatures. This is the table she uses to record her results:

Put the factor you are changing in the first column.

Use water at several different temperatures.

Temperature of water (°C)	Time to dissolve (seconds)
20	50
30	44
40	36
50	26
60	20

Remember to show what units you're using.

Use the second column to record how long it takes for the sugar to dissolve.

DISPLAYING RESULTS IN A LINE GRAPH

Line graphs are good for displaying the results of an experiment. You can draw a line graph when you have two sets of numbers.

Alesha's results are shown in this line graph:

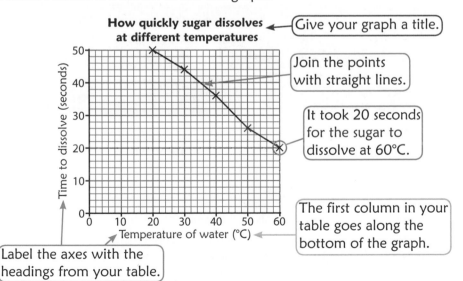

How quickly sugar dissolves at different temperatures

Give your graph a title.

Join the points with straight lines.

It took 20 seconds for the sugar to dissolve at 60°C.

The first column in your table goes along the bottom of the graph.

Label the axes with the headings from your table.

Scientific investigations

DISPLAYING RESULTS IN A BAR CHART

Bar charts are another good way to display the results of an experiment.
Laura dropped a tennis ball from a height of 1 metre onto different surfaces. The bar chart shows her results.

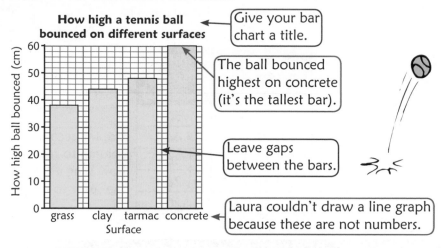

How high a tennis ball bounced on different surfaces ← Give your bar chart a title.

The ball bounced highest on concrete (it's the tallest bar).

Leave gaps between the bars.

Laura couldn't draw a line graph because these are not numbers.

WRITING A CONCLUSION

At the end of your investigation, you should write a sentence that sums up your results. This is called the conclusion. Here are some examples:

The hotter the water, the less time it takes for sugar to dissolve.

The harder the surface, the higher a tennis ball will bounce.

Your pulse rate goes up when you exercise.

The rougher the surface, the greater the friction.

Plants need water to grow, but too much kills them.

You should also write a sentence that starts 'I could have improved my investigation if I had ...' This is especially important if your experiment goes wrong!

QUICK QUIZ

1 How high did Laura's tennis ball bounce on **a** concrete? **b** grass?
2 Harry also investigates how high a ball bounces on different surfaces. He first bounces a football on grass. He then bounces a tennis ball on concrete. What is wrong with Harry's experiment?

Answers

LIVING THINGS

Page 2 Skeletons & muscles
1 Movement
2 Hollow bones are lighter so it's easier for birds to fly.

Page 3 Your heart
Sitting – 77 beats per minute
Walking – 95 beats per minute
Running – 127 beats per minute

Page 4 The digestive system
Mouth → Oesophagus → Stomach → Small intestine → Large intestine

Page 5 Teeth
1 Cow (Cows don't eat meat.)
2 False

Page 6 Keeping healthy
1 Bacteria will have all night to feed on the food and sugar left in your mouth. This causes tooth decay.
2 To avoid giving a disease to their patients.

Pages 7–8 Keeping healthy
1 a For example: orange, carrot
   b For example: green apple, peas
   c For example: banana, sweetcorn
   d For example: strawberry, red pepper
2 Kirsty should eat more fruit and vegetables.
3 False. Medicines are drugs that are used to treat or prevent diseases.

Page 9 Life cycles
Birth → Growth → Reproduction → Death

Page 10 Food chains
1 The arrows are going the wrong way.
2 Cabbage → Snail → Thrush

Page 11 Food chains
1 a Consumer   b Producer
2 False
3 False (Only animals can be prey.)

Page 12 Plants & growing conditions
1 False. A plant's leaves make its food.
2 It's too cold at the South Pole.

Page 13 How plants reproduce
The flower is pollinated by insects. It is brightly coloured to attract the insects.

Page 14 How plants reproduce
1 Fertilisation
2 To avoid overcrowding and give the new plants a better chance to grow and survive.

Page 15 How seeds grow into plants
A seed needs water, warmth and air to start growing. This process is called germination.

Page 16 Habitats
Camel – Desert – Long, thick eyelashes
Frog – Pond – Webbed feet
Polar bear – Arctic – Thick fur

Page 17 Evolution & inheritance
It will not survive to reproduce.

Page 18 Classification keys
1 Amphibian
2 A black mamba has teeth, is poisonous and doesn't live in water.

MATERIALS

Page 19 Rocks & soil
1 Chalk is permeable (lets water through) and wears away easily.
2 Chalk is softer than marble, so the rock that gets worn away must be chalk. Rock A is chalk. Rock B is marble.

Page 20 Rocks & fossils
The oldest layer is usually found at the bottom. Newer layers form on top.

Page 21 Conducting heat & electricity
1 Aluminium is a poor thermal insulator.
2 Plastic is a good electrical insulator (electricity won't flow through it). It stops you getting electrocuted.
3 Electricity can't flow through the wooden ruler, so the bulb would go out.

Page 22 Solids, liquids & gases
1 Vinegar is a liquid. Chalk and flour are solids. Helium is a gas.
2 False. Sugar, salt and rice can be poured.

Answers

MATERIALS

Page 23 Hot & cold
1 Bath water 38°C, ice lolly –2°C, glass of cold milk 5°C
2 Put a lid on it or put it in an insulated container, such as a Thermos flask.

Pages 24–25 Changing state
1 The chocolate melts.
2 Water turns to water vapour – Evaporation
Ice turns to water – Melting
Water vapour turns to water – Condensation
Water turns to ice – Freezing

Page 26 The water cycle
1 Water droplets
2 False

Page 27 Reversible & irreversible changes
Burning paper – irreversible
Melting chocolate – reversible
Dissolving sugar in water – reversible
Cooking bread – irreversible

Page 28 Separating mixtures of solids
1 First, remove the steel nails with a magnet. Then use a sieve to separate the flour and marbles.
2 The sand and salt would both go through the holes of the sieve.

Pages 29–30 Separating solids & liquids
1 Salt, sugar, instant coffee
2 Sugar and water – Evaporation
Flour and water – Filtering
Paper clips and marbles – Magnet
Marbles and water – Sieving
3 Add water so that the salt dissolves. Then filter the mixture to remove the sand. Finally, evaporate the water from the remaining salt solution to leave the salt.

PHYSICAL PROCESSES

Page 31 Electrical circuits
a There is no battery.
b There is a gap in the circuit.
c The wires should go to different ends of the battery.

Page 32 Circuit diagrams

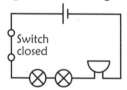

Switch closed

Pages 34–35 Sound & musical instruments
1 By touching or grabbing the cymbal to stop it vibrating.
2 No. There is no air to vibrate and carry the sound.
3 Drum B is the larger drum, so it has the lower pitch.

Pages 36–37 Light & seeing
1 True   2 False   3 False   4 False

Pages 38–39 Forces
B is easiest because the fulcrum is closest to the load.

Page 40 Forces
The rough surface gives more friction to stop you slipping over.

Page 41 Magnets & magnetic materials
The stronger magnet will pick up more paper clips. The stronger magnet will also attract the paper clips from further away.

Pages 42–43 The Earth & beyond
1 False. It takes a year.
2 False. The Sun is much bigger.
3 True

WORKING SCIENTIFICALLY

Pages 44–46 Scientific investigations
1 a 60 cm   b 38 cm

2 It is not a fair test. Harry has changed two factors, the type of ball and the surface.